My Secret Garden

And Other Poems for Children

Leeza Wilson

My Secret Garden and Other Poems for Children

© 2018 by Leeza Wilson

All rights reserved. No part of this book may be used or reproduced or transmitted in any form or by any means, electronic or mechanical, including photocopying, recording, or by any information storage and retrieval system, without written permission by the author except in the case of brief quotations embodied in critical articles or reviews.

Printed in the United States of America.

Edited and published by Tsarina Press

Pictures courtesy of Pixabay

ISBN: 978-1-948429-12-2

Table of Contents

My Secret Garden	1
Playful Words	3
Silly Sounds	4
Friends	5
A Stitch in Time	6
The Race	7
Emotions	8
Dear Time	9
Maybe	10
Spring	11
A Riddle	12
Figure Skating	14
My Weeping Willow	16
The Pecan Tree	17
Autumn Dawn	18
My Russia	19
The Willow	20
Hatfields and McCoys	22
Mr. Bunky	23
Back Porch Fantasies	24
Mr. Bunky and His Friend	26
Butterflies	27
Moonlit Bay	28
Flowers	29
The River's Bend	30
Fairies	31
The Eiffel Tower	32
Black Cat	33
Fall	34
A Child's Heart	35
Puddle Hopping	36
Hopscotch	38
A Counting Rhyme	40

Recess	41
Chocolate Milk and Cookies	42
Tugboat	43
Summer	44
The Friendship Bench	45
Summertime	46
Fireflies	47
Through the Looking Glass	48

My Secret Garden

Roses and Day Lilies

Poppies and Posies

Violets and Begonias

Oh, the delightful aromas

In my secret garden

Gardenias and Dahlias

Irises and Petunias

Anemones and Camellias

Oh, what beautiful flowers grow

In my secret garden

Hideaway trails sprinkled with flowers

And reading benches

Nestled in the trees

With hanging swings

No happier place to be

Than in my secret garden

Playful Words

Sweet tart

Differently alike

Upside down

Wrong side out

Round about

Gobbledygook

Weeble-wobble

Mollycoddle

Skedaddle

Snickerdoodle

Lickety-split

La-tee-da

Leeza Wilson

Silly Sounds

Flippity-flop

Hippity-hop

Topsy-turvy

Curvy-swervy

Woozy-doozy

Fuddy-duddy

Clickety-clack

Clackety-click

Smack

Thwack

Whack

Splish-splash

Plippity-plop

Friends

Dog has a friend

Who is a frog

Dog pounces

And frog bounces

Dog flops down

And frog hops up

Dog barks

And frog ribbits

Both play in the grass tidbits

Leeza Wilson

A Stitch in Time

Pretty in pink for
A stitch in time
To the ball we go
All three in a line

We'll eat and drink
And not stop to think
Just sing and dance
Like we're in France

The Race

Roaring engines

Pulsating in my ears

Rumbling pavement

Tickling my feet

Firing starter guns

Echoing through the air

Deafening screams of excited fans

As their favorite car wins

Emotions

Anger sounds like

The clashing symbols

Of a marching band

Madness looks like

A hurricane blowing

Across a mid-ocean island

Love smells like

Pink roses on

A summer's day

Sadness feels like

A coffin being

Lowered into a grave

Joy tastes like

Your very first

Piece of cake

Dear Time

Oh dear time,
Please allow me
These few lines
Just this one time.
For to me,
These lines are
Not just a rhyme
They are my lifeline.

Leeza Wilson

Maybe

Maybe strolls through
The swaying blades of hay.
Scythe in hand,
Maybe whacks away the day.
Maybe has very little to say,
Such is his way.
Maybe digs in the rock-hard clay.
Produce he hopes for in the coming days.
Maybe has a wife named Kay.
On the farm together
They will live all their life-long days.

Spring

Spring has sprung

A new world begun

Of rabbits hopping

And of flowers the rainbow popping

The trees are budding

The children running

In its warmth the sun embraces me

Enchanted I am by the singing bees

Fairies and sailboats in the skies

Drift by with whispering sighs

A Riddle

What do you hear

With your inner ear

When lines and rhymes

Of poetry dance and prance

While night becomes light?

Does the fright

To not be able to write

Leave you quaking in fear at night

That what you hear

With your inner ear

No one else ever will?

My Secret Garden

Figure Skating

Smooth, silvery ice
Glistening in the sunlight
Crisp breeze nipping at my nose
Like a ballerina
I strike a pose
And balance on my toes
I imagine a crowd
Watching me proud
I think of a song
One not too long
But with rhythm divine
With my body I form graceful lines
Performing my ballet on ice
With twirls and arabesque
Never more graceful have I been
Than when doing my program for pretend

My Secret Garden

My Weeping Willow

My weeping willow is a safe haven,
A hiding place from fears and troubles.
Under its drooping branches
Its feathery leaves conceal me from the world.
To another land I'm whisked away upon entering its dome
Where my childhood memories roam.
For inspiration it is my home.
My weeping willow cries in the rain.
Its tears wash away my pain.
When the sun is beating down
I feel not a ray.
My weeping willow shades me all day.
With a gentle breeze its boughs dance
In such a mesmerizing way.
And on a cold wintry day
It holds me in a warm embrace.
My beautiful weeping willow.

The Pecan Tree

Stretching into the heavens
Reaching out with its strong branches
Fluffed with leaves the yard it shades
And shields the swing from the sun's rays
The back porch it cools with wispy breezes
When the autumn comes, its fruit it rains
Covering the ground in a blanket of pecans
With glee we gather the loot
Filling pails to carry us the year through

Leeza Wilson

Autumn Dawn

Twinkling lights
Brightening the night
Flying by like
Shooting stars
Frost fading
On the windscreen
Emerging dawn veiling
The heavenly stars
Fog lifting from the
Crystal covered field
Daystar rising
Across the dawning sky
Through a shroud of fog
Peaks the mountain high
Over the rolling hills

My Russia

Rugged mountains dividing the realms
Tops covered in glistening snow
Under a thick gray sky the wild roams
Birches and brush blanketed in snow
Bright onion domes reaching into the heavens
Artic foxes peaking from their dens
A glint of sun through parting clouds
Icicles shimmering under the sun's rays
Colorful dachas painting the lands
Troikas racing through the snows
A masterpiece made by God's own hands

Leeza Wilson

The Willow

The willow,

Cool and shady

Are your embracing limbs

They shield me from

The ball of fire

High in the sky

In the cooling breeze

Your talent is seen

As your sinewy limbs

Gracefully dance in the wind

My Secret Garden

Leeza Wilson

Hatfields and McCoys

The Hatfields and McCoys
Their lives so full of ouches and oys
What reason is there for such noise?
They know not why
For what they fight
But each believes they are right
Have you ever seen such a sight
As two men dueling in the night?

Mr. Bunky

I have a horse

Whose name, of course,

Is Mr. Bunky

He lives in a barn

On a great big farm

Mr. Bunky has lots of charm

And warns the farmer when there's alarm

Back Porch Fantasies

My back porch
Is where I sit and daydream
And live out my fantasies
Free and fanciful
With fairytale endings

A powerful sea captain
I am one day
Sailing the high seas
On a mighty pirate ship

A doctor I will be another day,
In charge of my very own hospital
"She is so great!"
About me they will say

Then to my mansion I will return
Nestled away in a beautiful suburb
No need to open the windows
To enjoy the great outdoors
For if you look close
You will see, it's just my back porch

Leeza Wilson

Mr. Bunky and His Friend

Mr. Bunky

Is pretty spunky

He has a friend

Who is a monkey

And he's pretty funky

So if you happen to see Mr. Bunky

With his friend the monkey

Don't be shy

Just wave and say, "Hi!"

Butterflies

Butterflies, oh my!

So beautiful in the skies,

As on winds drift by.

Leeza Wilson

Moonlit Bay

At night on the bay,

The moonlight so calmly lays.

So serene I say.

My Secret Garden

Flowers

Tulips and daisies

In meadows so beautiful

Dancing in the sun

Leeza Wilson

The River's Bend

At the river's bend

Where the mountains touch the sky

My paradise lies

Fairies

Fairies on tulips

Dancing in the warm spring breeze

With shimmering wings

Leeza Wilson

The Eiffel Tower

The Eiffel Tower
Warming the fall night in lights
Moon remains behind

Black Cat

Cat as black as night
Fall leaves rustling under feet
Moon rising up high

Fall

Full moon in the sky

Fog forming over the ground

Pumpkins on porches

A Child's Heart

A child's heart

Innocent and pure

No greater love can come

Than from a child's heart

Everyone is at home

In a child's heart

The love is unconditional and true

And is deeper than the ocean blue

Within a child's heart

Leeza Wilson

Puddle Hopping

Summer days bring long hours of play
But nothing squashes the fun
Quite like a thunderstorm
My friend and I wait
With impatient stares
At the falling rain
We watch the water
As it flows down the steps
Making puddles at the bottom of the gutters
"Let's go puddle hopping!" we say
As soon as the thunder stops
Out the door we go
Stomping and hopping
In puddles as we go our way
To the street to puddle hop
Splish-splash

In the water in the curb we hop

Puddle hopping

Puddle hopping

No better fun than puddle hopping

Leeza Wilson

Hopscotch

Hopscotch at recess
Hopscotch at home
Hopscotch with friends
Hopscotch alone
Hopscotch in summer and
Hopscotch in winter
Hopscotch the whole year long
There's nothing I like better than
Hopscotch!

A Counting Rhyme

One, two

You're my honeydew

Three, four

I couldn't love you more

Five, Six

You're cuter than baby chicks

Seven, eight

You're just GREAT!

Recess

Recess

Exercise at its best

Children running and screaming

Everywhere laughing and playing

Studies on pause

Students for a moment without a cause

Leeza Wilson

Chocolate Milk and Cookies

Chocolate milk and cookies

My favorite treat to eat

And when they're warm

They're so chewy and delicious

Around them we all swarm

Tugboat

Toot! Toot!

Goes the tugboat

In my tub it floats

Bobbing along on handmade waves

Looking for the next victim to save

Toot! Toot!

Goes the tugboat

Leeza Wilson

Summer

Summer brings all the fun

Under the sun

Make-believe play

That lasts all day

Making memories with friends

That'll never fade

Every night staying up late

Roaming the world

Of imagination by day

The Friendship Bench

Everyone needs a friend

No matter if you're big or small

No matter if you're short or tall

No matter if your skin is fair or dark

We all need a friend

Without a friend,

The world can seem stark

So there's a special bench

In our city park

If you're lonely,

Bullied, or just shy

You can sit on the friendship bench

And someone will sit with you

And say, "Hi!"

Because everyone deserves a friend

And a friend is only a bench away

Leeza Wilson

Summertime

Ladybugs and daffodils
Jumping frogs on lily pads
Fireflies and fairy tales
Butterflies and lilies
Spiders spinning webs
Bunnies hopping in the fields
Grasshoppers playing in the grass
Crickets chirping little tunes
Summer's little beauties

Fireflies

Ten thousand fireflies
Giving little hugs of light
To the summer's night
We'll chase them for hours
Hoping to catch a few in jars
What a most delightful prize
To have our own fireflies
Watching their twinkling lights
Brings so much delight

Leeza Wilson

Through the Looking Glass

Through the looking glass
Lives my secret friends
They're the cutest you've ever seen
They only come out for kids
And only if you believe
They are short and fuzzy
With crazy, wild hair
They come in a rainbow of colors
They are super polite
And teach that sharing is right
They love to give hugs
They hug you so tight
With all their might
They love *all* kids
All over the world
And truly know that love
Is the power that makes the world turn

About the Author

Leeza grew up with a fascination for notebooks and writing utensils. She began reading and writing at age four, mostly self-taught due to her independent and determined personality. She has had a love of books and reading her entire life. And from her love of reading has grown a love of writing. She enjoys writing stories that embrace the human psyche and relate the joys and struggles that we each face, and how we live through those moments. She writes in the genres of romance, mystery, suspense, historical, literary fiction, poetry, and children's.

When not writing, she enjoys drawing and painting; spending time with her family; listening to music; volunteering with her local fire department as a firefighter and EMT-Advanced; and playing the piano and guitar. She lives with her son, two cats, and Chihuahua in the Smoky Mountains of Tennessee.

Follow Leeza on Social Media

www.facebook.com/icanbeahero

www.twitter.com/leezatheauthor

www.instagram.com/leezatheauthor

www.facebook.com/leezatheauthor

Other books By Leeza Wilson

My Grandpa is Extra Sweet: Diabetic Emergencies
The Germ Squad: Colds, Flu, and Stomach Bugs
Where is Your Heartbeat? Cardiac Emergencies (coming soon)
A Bouquet of Poems

Please Write a Review

Thank you for reading my book. It is my deepest wish that you had a pleasant reading experience and found the story enjoyable. Whether you did or didn't, please feel free to get in touch and let me know what you thought. I love hearing from my readers and I always try my best to respond to emails and social media messages from my fans.

As any author will tell you, reviews are so very important in helping our books get noticed. Reviews help authors reach more readers by letting them know if a book is worth reading or not. So I rely a lot on reviews to help readers find my books and know if they're worthy of investing their time in to read. It only takes a couple of minutes to write a brief review of what you thought of the book. So if you can take a minute to write an honest review, I would greatly appreciate it, even if it's a negative review. All reviews matter, whether they're 1 star or 5 stars, a small essay or just one word. I value your honest feedback.

Thanks!

Leeza Wilson

www.ingramcontent.com/pod-product-compliance
Lightning Source LLC
Chambersburg PA
CBHW041314110526
44591CB00022B/2912